Children's Prayers to Thank God for His Blessings

CHILDREN'S CHRISTIAN PRAYER BOOKS

BABY PROFESSOR
EDUCATION KIDS

Speedy Publishing LLC

40 E. Main St. #1156

Newark, DE 19711

www.speedypublishing.com

Copyright 2016

All Rights reserved. No part of this book may be reproduced or used in any way or form or by any means whether electronic or mechanical, this means that you cannot record or photocopy any material ideas or tips that are provided in this book

Everything we see in this world is from God. He is the source of every blessing that we receive and so we should thank Him every day. The way to talk to him is through prayer.

Prayers traditionally end with "amen". This is from the Hebrew word for "it is true" or "so be it".

Here are sample prayers for children to use:

A Short Prayer of Thanksgiving

Dear and gracious Lord, we thank you
For the light that shines each new morning,
For shelter and rest in the night,
For the food that we eat to nourish our bodies,
For the love of friends and family members,
For everything you have sent for our goodness.

Prayer to Thank God for our Family

Our most loving Father God,
I pray for my family to have
Faith to work out our differences and become united,
Grace that helps us care for one another and celebrate together,
Faith that we will overcome adversities and come out triumphant,
Love that will guide us to envision our future together and as individuals,
Faith that we can find love and peace in this troubled world.
I trust that you will always care and watch over us. Amen.

Prayer to Thank God for Meals

God is great and God is good,
And we thank Him for our food;
By God's grace we now are fed,
Thank God for our daily bread. Amen.

Prayer for Mornings

Now before I run outside and play,
Let me not forget to thank you for this new day
And for keeping me safe through the night,
And for waking me with this morning light.
Please be with me through this day,
In my work and in my play. Amen.

Bedtime Prayer

Now I lay myself to sleep
I pray the Lord my soul to keep;
Keep me safe all through the night,
And wake me with the morning light.
Amen.

Practice Writing Exercises

Trace the Prayer below.

A SHORT PRAYER OF THANKSGIVING

Dear and gracious Lord, we thank you
For the light that shines each
new morning,
For shelter and rest in the night,
For the food that we eat to nourish
our bodies,
For the love of friends and family
members,
For everything you have sent for
our goodness.

Write your own Thanksgiving Prayer here

Trace the Prayer below.

PRAYER TO THANK GOD FOR OUR FAMILY

Our most loving Father God,
I pray for my family to have
Faith to work out our
differences and become united,
Grace that helps us care for
one another and celebrate
together,
Faith that we will overcome

Trace the Prayer below.

adversities and come out
triumphant,
Love that will guide us to
envision our future together
and as individuals,
Faith that we can find love and
peace in this troubled world.
I trust that you will always
care and watch over us. Amen.

Write your own "Prayer to thank God for our family" here

Write your own Prayer before going to School.

Trace the Prayer below.

PRAYER TO THANK GOD FOR MEALS

God is great and God is good,
And we thank Him for our food;
By God's grace we now are fed,
Thank God for our daily bread.
Amen.

Write your own "Prayer to Thank God for Meals" here

Trace the Prayer below.

PRAYER FOR MORNINGS

Now before I run outside and play,
Let me not forget to thank you
for this new day
And for keeping me safe through
the night,
And for waking me with this
morning light.
Please be with me through this day,
In my work and in my play. Amen.

Write your own "Prayer for Mornings" Prayer here

Trace the Prayer below.

BEDTIME PRAYER

Now I lay myself to sleep
I pray the Lord my soul to keep;
Keep me safe all through the night,
And wake me with the
morning light.
Amen.

Write your own "Bedtime Prayer" Prayer here

Trace the Prayer below.

A SHORT PRAYER
OF THANKSGIVING

Dear and gracious Lord, we thank you
For the light that shines each new
morning,
For shelter and rest in the night,
For the food that we eat to nourish our bodies,
For the love of friends and family members,
For everything you have sent for our
goodness.

Rewrite the prayer here.

Trace the Prayer below.

PRAYER TO THANK GOD FOR OUR FAMILY

Our most loving Father God,
I pray for my family to have
Faith to work out our differences
and become united,
Grace that helps us care for one
another and celebrate together,

Rewrite the prayer here.

Trace the Prayer below.

Faith that we will overcome adversities and come out triumphant,
Love that will guide us to envision our future together and as individuals,
Faith that we can find love and peace in this troubled world.
I trust that you will always care and watch over us. Amen.

Rewrite the prayer here.

Trace the Prayer below.

PRAYER TO THANK GOD FOR MEALS

God is great and God is good,
And we thank Him for our food;
By God's grace we now are fed,
Thank God for our daily bread. Amen.

PRAYER FOR MORNINGS

Now before I run outside and play,
Let me not forget to thank you for
this new day

Rewrite the prayer here.

Trace the Prayer below.

And for keeping me safe through the night,
And for waking me with this morning light.
Please be with me through this day,
In my work and in my play. Amen.

BEDTIME PRAYER

Now I lay myself to sleep
I pray the Lord my soul to keep;
Keep me safe all through the night,
And wake me with the morning light.
Amen.

Rewrite the prayer here.

Lightning Source UK Ltd.
Milton Keynes UK
UKHW052018060121
376558UK00006B/31